ITALY

MORE THAN JUST A JOURNEY

FRANCO MARZELLA

© 2023 [Franco Marzella].

All rights reserved. No part of this publication may be reproduced, distributed, or transmitted in any form or by any means, including photocopying, recording, or other electronic or mechanical methods, without the prior written permission of the publisher, except in the case of brief quotations embodied in critical reviews and certain other noncommercial uses permitted by copyright law.

Book Design by Aeyshaa

*To all who dream of Italy,
and to Italy herself,
for enchanting us all.*

CONTENTS

Why This Book? 5
01. Introduction to Italy 7
02. Italian Cuisine 11
03. Italian Art and Architecture 15
04. Transportation and Travel Logistics 19
05. Tuscany - Florence and Siena 23
06. Lombardy - Milan and the Lakes 30
07. Veneto - Venice and Verona 35
08. Lazio - Rome: The Eternal City 40
09. Campania - Naples, Pompeii, and
 the Amalfi Coast 45
10. Liguria - Cinque Terre and Portofino 52
11. Emilia-Romagna - Bologna and Modena 57
12. Piedmont - Turin and the Wine Country 62
13. Sicily - Palermo and the Ancient Ruins 68
14. Puglia - Bari and the Adriatic Coast 75
15. The Grape Escape: Wines of Italy and Their
 Pairings 79
16. Building Your Itinerary - Tailoring Your Italian
 Adventure 85
17. Travel Etiquette - Navigating Italy with Grace and
 Respect 88
18. Useful Italian Phrases - Communicating with
 Locals 92
19. Italy Unleashed – Embrace the Outdoors 96
20. La Dolce Vita - Nightlife in Italy 100
21. Unique Italian Experiences - Beyond
 Sightseeing 104
22. Arrivederci, Italy - Final Thoughts 107

About the Author 110

WHY THIS BOOK?

Stroll down any travel aisle in your local bookstore and you'll be inundated with guidebooks on Italy. You'll see glossy, hardcover anthologies that could double as free-weights, chock full of historical timelines and architectural blueprints. And while there's no denying the beauty of the Sistine Chapel or the splendor of Pompeii, the question remains - do you really want to explore Italy like it's a pop quiz?

I, your humble author, Franco Marzella, certainly didn't think so. That's why "Italy: More than Just a Journey" was born. This guidebook isn't your typical tourist handbook, not by a long shot. It's the must-have companion for the travelers who want to experience Italy, not just see it. We're talking about immersing oneself in the local culture, cuisine, and customs like an authentic Italian. Or at least, like an authentic Italian-American pharmacist-turned-travel guide author. Which is where I come in.

As a second-generation Italian-American, my roots are firmly planted in the rich soil of Sicily and Rome, and my passport is peppered with Italian stamps. I've dined with Milanese fashionistas, gotten lost in Palermo's bustling markets, debated the true recipe for carbonara with Roman nonnas, and chased down rogue buses in rural Tuscany. And now, I'm ready to pass all that wisdom (and some would say, mischief) onto you.

With this book, you're not just getting the run-of-the-mill tourist checklist. Oh no, dear friend, this guide delves deeper. We'll go beyond the well-trodden path, explore the backstreets, live the traditions, and taste the gastronomic wonders from the Alps to the Aeolian Islands. This is about discovering the true heart of Italy, one adventure at a time.

So, why this book? Because Italy is more than just the Colosseum and canals, pizza and pasta, fashion and Ferrari. It's an unforgettable adventure, a captivating story, and a personal journey all in one. And with this guide in hand, your Italian journey will be all that and more.

Are you ready? Andiamo! Let's go!

CHAPTER 1
INTRODUCTION TO ITALY

Welcome to Italy, a country that is as diverse as it is captivating. This peninsula, nestled in the heart of the Mediterranean Sea, is a treasure trove of art, history, culture, and gastronomy that allures travelers from around the world. But Italy offers more than just a trip; it offers an immersive experience that can transform the way we see and understand the world.

Italy is a patchwork of regions, each boasting its unique charm and character. From the sun-soaked landscapes of the south to the snowy alpine peaks of the north, every journey across its territories is a trip through time, where centuries of history unfold before your eyes. Here, the ancient relics of the Roman Empire coexist with the architectural wonders of the Renaissance, and the avant-garde design of the present times.

The country's illustrious past lives on in its diverse culture. As the cradle of the Roman civilization and the birthplace of the Renaissance, Italy has profoundly influenced the world's development in art, architecture, and science. This rich heritage is visible in every corner of the country, from the Colosseum of Rome to the elegant palaces of Venice, from the Duomo of Florence to the historic city center of Naples.

But Italy is not just about the past; it is a vibrant and dynamic country, where tradition and modernity blend seamlessly. The bustling fashion capital of Milan showcases Italy's flair for design and innovation, while the tech industries of Turin and the Emilia-Romagna region underscore its cutting-edge contributions to the global economy.

The Italian lifestyle, encapsulated in the philosophy of 'La Dolce Vita,' or 'The Sweet Life,' is a major part of its allure. This manifests in a myriad of ways - from the unhurried afternoons spent savoring a cup of espresso, to the evenings filled with lively conversation around a family dinner table. Food and wine play a crucial role in Italian culture, with regional cuisines and local vineyards contributing to an envious gastronomical diversity.

Whether it is the seductive allure of Rome, the rustic charm of Tuscany, the scenic beauty of the Amalfi Coast, or the culinary delights of Emilia-Romagna, Italy's offerings are as varied as they are plentiful.

Traveling to Italy also means discovering its people, whose warmth, passion, and creativity are the very essence of the country. Their rich traditions, enduring customs, and spirit of 'bella figura' — presenting oneself in the best possible way — reflect a culture that values beauty, style, and the joy of living.

Yet, the real Italy is found beyond the well-trodden tourist paths. It's in the sleepy hill towns, the bustling local markets, the family-run vineyards, and the traditional festivals that you'll uncover the country's soul.

In this book, we'll guide you through Italy's most celebrated regions, exploring their highlights and hidden gems, and providing practical advice to help you plan your journey. But remember, no book can capture all of Italy's magic. That's a journey you'll have to make for yourself. Here's to Italy — a country that not only inspires but also transforms.

Where the Tiber River meets the magnificent St. Peter's Basilica, a captivating scene unfolds, capturing the essence of beauty and history.

CHAPTER 2
ITALIAN CUISINE

Italian cuisine, with its intoxicating aromas, fresh flavors, and rich traditions, often sparks an irresistible allure. Famed for its wide-ranging gastronomy, from artisanal pizzas and handmade pasta to aromatic espresso and robust wines, the culinary treasures of Italy have captivated palates across the world.

At the core of Italian cuisine lies the philosophy of 'less is more,' with an emphasis on fresh, high-quality ingredients. The nation's gastronomic heritage embodies the essence of its geographic and cultural diversity, with each region and even towns within the same province, boasting their own unique specialties and culinary techniques.

Before we embark on a culinary exploration of each region, it's crucial to understand how an Italian meal is traditionally structured:

1. **Antipasto (Starter):** This is the first course, which can be a cold or hot dish, and may include a variety of meats, cheeses, olives, and marinated vegetables.

2. **Primo (First Course):** This course typically consists of a hot dish like pasta, risotto, gnocchi, or soup.

3. **Secondo (Second Course):** The main course, the secondo is typically a meat or fish dish, served alongside a side dish or "contorno."
4. **Contorno (Side Dish):** This is usually a vegetable dish that can be served with the secondo.
5. **Dolce (Dessert):** Sweets to end the meal, which can range from pastries and cakes to gelato or fruit.
6. **Caffè & Digestivo:** The meal is rounded off with an espresso (caffè) and a digestivo, a digestive liquor like limoncello, grappa, or amaro.

In the sun-drenched south, with regions like Campania and Sicily, the kitchen is bright with the tastes of ripe tomatoes, virgin olive oil, fresh seafood, and sun-ripened fruits and vegetables. Pizza, hailing from Naples, has become a global symbol of Italian cuisine, celebrated for its thin, slightly charred crust adorned with San Marzano tomatoes, mozzarella cheese, fresh basil, and a drizzle of olive oil.

In the northern regions such as Lombardy, Piedmont, and Emilia-Romagna, the cuisine embraces a rich and indulgent character. Known for butter-based cooking, the liberal use of creams and cheeses, and an array of dishes like risottos and stuffed pasta, these areas are a haven for comfort food lovers.

The heartland of Italy, with regions like Tuscany and Umbria, prides itself on its "cucina povera" or "peasant cooking," making the most of local products to create robust, earthy dishes. Tuscan bread, steak Florentine, and the region's sublime olive oil have garnered worldwide recognition.

Coastal regions shine with seafood-centric dishes, such as Veneto's creamy risotto di mare or Liguria's trofie al pesto paired with fresh seafood. To complement the vast spectrum of dishes, Italy also boasts a diverse range of wines, from Piedmont's robust Barolo, Veneto's crisp white Soave, to Tuscany's deep red Chianti and Brunello di Montalcino.

The final notes of an Italian feast are often sweet, marked by delectable desserts like creamy gelato, sweet ricotta-filled cannoli, and the holiday staple, panettone. No overview of Italian cuisine can be complete without acknowledging the importance of its coffee culture - a cherished daily ritual.

In Italy, food transcends beyond the confines of the kitchen. It's a celebration of life, a reason for families to gather, and an intrinsic part of festivals and seasons, with specific dishes marking different times of the year. As you navigate through the culinary landscape of Italy's most beloved regions in this book, remember that the beauty of Italian cuisine lies in its simplicity and the respect for quality ingredients. As the Italians say, "La semplicità è l'ultima sofisticazione" - "Simplicity is the ultimate sophistication". So, prepare yourself for a delightful gastronomic adventure. Buon appetito - enjoy your meal!

Indulge in a delightful feast of wine and cuisine while savoring the picturesque view of Lake Como.

CHAPTER 3
ITALIAN ART AND ARCHITECTURE

Italy's rich tapestry of art and architecture is nothing short of breathtaking. The country is a vast, open-air museum where every street, square, and building whispers tales from an opulent past. With more UNESCO World Heritage Sites than any other country in the world, Italy stands as a testament to thousands of years of cultural and artistic evolution.

Art

The Italian peninsula has been the birthplace and canvas for numerous artistic movements that have shaped global culture. This journey begins with the ancient Roman civilization, whose sculptures, frescoes, and mosaics showcased remarkable realism and narrative detail. A visit to Rome's Capitoline Museums or the preserved cities of Pompeii and Herculaneum offers a glimpse into this era's artistic prowess.

The Middle Ages saw the rise of religiously inspired art, with Byzantine mosaics adorning Italy's churches, particularly in Ravenna. The Romanesque and Gothic periods that followed gave us towering cathedrals and churches such as the Modena Cathedral and Orvieto Cathedral, where art and faith intertwined.

The Renaissance, a period of renewed interest in classical ideals and a focus on humanism, originated in Italy in the 14th century. Florence, often referred to as the cradle of the Renaissance, became a powerhouse of art and culture. Great masters like Leonardo da Vinci, Michelangelo, and Raphael created some of the world's most iconic works, including 'The Last Supper,' 'David,' and the frescoes of the Sistine Chapel.

Later, the Baroque period would produce grand and dramatic art and architecture, marked by elaborate details and a sense of movement. Works by artists like Caravaggio, Bernini, and Borromini, such as the 'Ecstasy of Saint Teresa' and 'St. Peter's Basilica,' encapsulate this era's spirit.

Italy's contribution to the art world continued into the modern and contemporary periods, with movements like Futurism, Arte Povera, and Transavantgarde. Artists such as Modigliani, Morandi, Fontana, and Cattelan have carried Italy's artistic legacy into the present day.

Architecture

Italy's architectural styles are as diverse as its art. From the engineering marvels of the Roman Empire, including the Colosseum, the Pantheon, and the aqueducts, to the gravity-defying domes and bell towers of the Middle Ages and Renaissance, Italy's built environment is a chronicle of its history.

The harmonious proportions of Palladio's villas in the Veneto region and the elegant symmetry of the

High Renaissance architecture in the cities of Florence, Rome, and Milan speak of an era when architecture was considered the 'mother of all arts'. The grand piazzas and palaces, adorned with intricate details, as seen in Turin, Rome, or Lecce's baroque city center, exude opulence and grandeur.

More recently, Italy has contributed to modernist and contemporary architecture with the works of architects like Gio Ponti, Renzo Piano, and Zaha Hadid. Italy's architectural language continues to evolve, embracing sustainable practices and cutting-edge design.

Throughout this guide, as we journey through Italy's various regions, you'll discover the remarkable art and architectural gems that each has to offer. We'll guide you through museums, churches, palaces, and modern landmarks, highlighting not-to-be-missed works and providing context to deepen your appreciation of these masterpieces. After all, understanding Italy's art and architecture is key to unlocking the country's soul.

Discover the allure of Palermo, Sicily, through the enchanting Piazza Pretoria, where history and beauty unite in an unforgettable embrace

CHAPTER 4
TRANSPORTATION AND TRAVEL LOGISTICS

Traveling in Italy can be a rewarding experience, filled with awe-inspiring sights, rich culture, and gastronomic delights. To fully enjoy your journey, it's crucial to understand the country's transportation systems and travel logistics.

Air Travel

Italy is well-served by international and domestic flights. Major international gateways include Leonardo da Vinci–Fiumicino Airport in Rome and Malpensa Airport in Milan. Other significant airports are found in Venice, Naples, Bologna, and Pisa. Low-cost airlines and traditional carriers operate domestic flights that can save time when traveling between regions.

Train Travel

Italy has an extensive and reliable train network run mainly by Trenitalia, the state-owned company, and Italo, a private operator. The high-speed trains, 'Frecciarossa' and 'Italo,' connect major cities like Rome, Milan, Florence, Venice, and Naples, reducing travel times significantly. Slower regional trains provide a more economical option, connecting smaller towns and offering scenic routes. Remember to validate your ticket before boarding regional trains to avoid fines.

Bus Travel

While train travel is usually preferable for intercity connections, buses serve areas that are not easily accessible by train, especially in the southern regions and some mountainous areas. Bus travel is also prevalent in cities and towns, with tickets typically purchased at tobacco shops, newsstands, or automated machines.

Car Travel

Renting a car provides the most flexibility, especially for exploring the countryside or smaller towns where public transportation is limited. However, driving in Italy may present challenges for the uninitiated, including heavy traffic, limited parking, and restricted traffic zones (ZTLs) in many historical city centers.

International and local car rental companies are available at most airports and city centers. Remember, an International Driving Permit is required along with your driver's license.

Boat Travel

Italy, with its extensive coastline and islands, offers numerous ferry services. Major routes include connections to the islands of Sardinia and Sicily, as well as services along the Amalfi Coast and the islands of the Bay of Naples. Venice, the city of canals, provides a unique boat travel experience with its vaporettos (water buses) and iconic gondolas.

Travel Logistics

Accommodation in Italy ranges from high-end luxury hotels to budget-friendly hostels and charming bed-and-breakfasts. Booking in advance is recommended, especially in peak tourist seasons.

It's essential to be aware of the Italian concept of 'riposo', a midday break when many shops and restaurants close, usually between 1 PM and 4 PM.

The currency in Italy is the Euro, and credit cards are widely accepted. Still, it's always useful to carry some cash for small expenses, particularly in smaller towns or for tipping, which is appreciated but not mandatory.

Finally, consider investing in a travel insurance policy that covers medical expenses, trip cancellations, and loss of belongings. The emergency number in Italy, as in all of Europe, is 112.

Understanding these practical aspects will ensure a smoother, more enjoyable journey through the beauty and diversity that is Italy. Your Italian adventure awaits!

"Down the rabbit hole of Italy's magic: cobblestone paths weaving a captivating tale of history and charm."

CHAPTER 5
TUSCANY - FLORENCE AND SIENA

Welcome to Tuscany, the birthplace of the Renaissance and the epitome of romantic Italy. Tuscany is renowned for its idyllic landscapes of rolling hills, cypress-lined country roads, sprawling vineyards, and charming medieval hill towns. This region offers a perfect blend of rich history, artistic legacy, culinary traditions, and natural beauty. With its capital, Florence, and the historic city of Siena at its heart, Tuscany promises a journey through time and culture that will captivate your senses.

History

Tuscany's history is layered with Etruscan roots, Roman rule, Medieval warfare, and Renaissance blossoming. The region was the heartland of the Etruscans, an advanced civilization that greatly influenced Roman culture. Post-Roman rule, Tuscany saw periods of conflict, including wars between Guelphs and Ghibellines, and between rival cities. The Renaissance marked an era of prosperity and artistic flourish, with the Medici family of Florence at the forefront, acting as patrons of artists, scholars, and architects.

Cultural Highlights

Tuscan culture is an enchanting mix of tradition, history, and 'la dolce vita.' Its language, Tuscan dialect, formed the basis of modern Italian. Traditional festivals, such as Siena's Palio, a thrilling horse race, or Florence's colorful 'Scoppio del Carro' at Easter, keep local customs alive. Tuscany has given the world literary greats like Dante, Petrarch, and Boccaccio, and its music traditions range from the classical compositions of Puccini to popular folk tunes.

Major Cities and Attractions

Florence

- **Sights**: Florence, the region's capital, is a treasure trove of world-class art and architecture. Start with the iconic Cattedrale di Santa Maria del Fiore, or the Duomo, a symbol of Florence with its distinctive red-tiled dome that offers panoramic views of the city. A few steps away, the Baptistery of St. John boasts beautiful mosaics and the famous bronze Gates of Paradise.

  Cross the River Arno via the Ponte Vecchio, a Medieval stone bridge lined with jewelry shops. On the other side lies the Pitti Palace, a Renaissance palace hosting an extensive collection of paintings, sculptures, and royal apartments.

  Visit the Uffizi Gallery, one of the world's most famous art museums, where masterpieces by Botticelli, Leonardo da Vinci, Michelangelo, and others are on display. For more of Michelangelo, head to the Galleria dell'Accademia to witness the majestic statue of David. Finish your day with a scenic view of the city from the hilltop Piazzale Michelangelo.

- **Local Cuisine**: Florentine cuisine is characterized by its simplicity and the quality of its local ingredients. Try 'bistecca alla fiorentina', a T-bone steak sourced from local Chianina cattle, grilled over hot coals and traditionally served rare. The 'ribollita' is a heartwarming bread and vegetable soup, a symbol of Tuscan peasant cooking. Taste the 'pappa al pomodoro', a rich tomato and bread soup. For something lighter, try 'panzanella', a refreshing bread salad with tomatoes and basil.

  Florentine street food includes 'lampredotto', a sandwich made with the fourth stomach of a cow, a delicacy for the adventurous. Finish your meal with 'cantucci e vin santo', almond cookies dunked in sweet wine. For gelato lovers, Florence is the birthplace of this delectable dessert, and numerous gelaterias offer a wide array of flavors.

- **Shopping**: Florence is famed for its leather goods and artisanal crafts. Explore the San Lorenzo Market for leather jackets and the Ponte Vecchio for unique jewelry.

- **Accommodation**: Florence offers a range of accommodations, from luxurious hotels along the Arno river to quaint bed-and-breakfasts in the historic center.

Siena

- **Sights**: Siena, a well-preserved medieval city, is known for its stunning architectural sights. Begin with the Piazza del Campo, one of Europe's greatest medieval squares and the site of the Palio horse race. The square's unique shell shape is divided into nine sectors, representing the Nine Lords of the Sienese Government. At one end of the square stands the Palazzo Pubblico, with its tall bell tower, Torre del Mangia. Visitors can climb the tower for an unforgettable view of Siena and the surrounding Tuscan countryside.

The Siena Cathedral is a stunning example of Italian Romanesque-Gothic architecture, with its striking black and white facade. Inside, intricate mosaics adorn the floors, and the Piccolomini Library showcases vibrant frescoes. Don't miss the Baptistery and the adjacent Museo dell'Opera del Duomo, which houses works by Duccio, Donatello, and others.

- **Local Cuisine**: Sienese cuisine offers a delightful mix of flavors. Try 'pici', a thick, hand-rolled pasta, typically served with garlic or a meaty ragù. The 'cinta senese', a local pork breed, is used in various dishes, including salamis and prosciutto. 'Panforte', a dense, spiced fruitcake with honey and nuts, is a Sienese specialty, as is 'ricciarelli', soft almond cookies often enjoyed during Christmas. For a unique taste, sample 'pappa al pomodoro' or 'ribollita', both hearty Tuscan soups featuring bread and locally grown vegetables.
- **Shopping**: Siena's medieval streets are perfect for shopping, with local ceramics, terracotta, and traditional sweets like 'ricciarelli' being popular choices.
- **Accommodation**: Siena has charming boutique hotels within medieval buildings and affordable guesthouses in its winding streets.

Outdoor Activities

Tuscany's varied landscapes offer excellent hiking, cycling, and horseback riding. The Chianti region, stretching between Florence and Siena, offers unforgettable wine-tasting tours.

Transportation

Both Florence and Siena are well-connected by train and bus networks. Within the cities, walking is the best way to explore. Consider renting a car for day trips to the countryside, keeping in mind ZTL restrictions in city centers.

Practical Information

Tuscans are friendly but appreciate formal manners. In restaurants, 'coperto' (a service charge) is common. The climate is typically Mediterranean, with hot summers and mild winters, and the peak tourist season is summer, although spring and fall see fewer crowds and pleasant weather.

Sample Itinerary

Day 1-3: Explore Florence's art and architecture, including the Uffizi, the Accademia, and the Duomo. Visit local markets and enjoy Tuscan cuisine.

Day 4: Take a day trip to the Chianti region for wine tasting.

Day 5-6: Discover Siena's medieval charm, visit the Cathedral, and explore Piazza del Campo.

Day 7: Visit San Gimignano or Pisa for a day trip, or unwind in one of Tuscany's thermal baths, like those in Montecatini Terme.

Tuscany, with its mesmerizing landscapes, rich artistic heritage, and delectable cuisine, promises a captivating journey that will linger in your memories long after you've left its sun-drenched hills.

Insider Info: Tuscany - Florence and Siena

- Tuscany is home to seven UNESCO World Heritage Sites, including the historic centers of Florence and Siena.
- The iconic landscape of Val d'Orcia in Tuscany has been captured in numerous works of art throughout history, making it one of the most painted landscapes in the world.
- In Florence, the local dialect of Italian is actually the standard form of the language taught worldwide.

Insider's Extras

Downloading the TrenItalia and Italo apps: Traveling by train is a quintessential Italian experience. Keep all your tickets handy and access real-time updates by downloading the TrenItalia and Italo apps. You can buy train tickets in advance, avoid lines, bypass broken machines at stations, and access digital-only discounts. It's a smarter way to traverse Italy's vast rail network.

Taking high-speed trains: For inter-city travels, high-speed trains are a lifesaver. They're typically available on primary routes and are often faster, more comfortable, and provide more scenic views than flying. Ensure to book these in advance during peak tourist seasons.

Witness the breathtaking Cathedral of Florence as it proudly dominates the city's skyline.

CHAPTER 6
LOMBARDY - MILAN AND THE LAKES

Lombardy, in the northern part of Italy, is an enticing mix of bustling cities, serene lakes, and magnificent alpine landscapes. Its capital, Milan, is a global hub for fashion and design, while the serene lakes like Como and Garda are a soothing escape from the urban tempo. In Lombardy, the contemporary and the traditional blend harmoniously, promising an enriching experience.

History

Historically, Lombardy has been a center of power and trade. It was part of the Roman Empire, later became a key player in the Holy Roman Empire, and saw a period of prosperity under the Sforza family during the Renaissance. Milan was also a focal point during the unification of Italy. The region's historical layers have shaped its diverse and distinct cultural heritage.

Cultural Highlights

Lombardy's culture is a rich tapestry woven through its history, traditions, and contemporary trends. The region has contributed significantly to music, being home to the world-renowned La Scala opera house. Lombardy's calendar is dotted with festivals like the Milan Fashion Week and the Festa del Naviglio.

Major Cities and Attractions

Milan

- **Sights**: Milan is a city of glamour, history, and art. Start at the Duomo di Milano, one of the world's largest cathedrals, with its stunning gothic architecture. Climb to the rooftop for panoramic views of the city. Near the cathedral, Galleria Vittorio Emanuele II, one of the oldest shopping malls, is a spectacle with its glass-vaulted arcades.

  Visit the Convent of Santa Maria delle Grazie, which houses Leonardo da Vinci's "The Last Supper", one of the most famous artworks in the world. Explore Castello Sforzesco, a massive castle with museums and art collections, including works by Michelangelo and da Vinci.

  Take a stroll in the trendy district of Brera, home to the Pinacoteca di Brera, which showcases a comprehensive collection of Italian Renaissance art. End your day in the Navigli District, famous for its canals, boutiques, and buzzing nightlife.

- **Local Cuisine**: Milanese cuisine is hearty and varied. Try the 'cotoletta alla Milanese', a breaded veal cutlet fried in butter, and 'risotto alla Milanese', a creamy rice dish cooked with saffron. 'Cassoeula', a warming pork and cabbage stew, is perfect for colder months. For dessert, enjoy 'panettone', a sweet bread loaf with raisins and candied orange, typically enjoyed during Christmas.

The Lakes

- **Sights**: Lombardy's lakes are known for their picturesque beauty. Lake Como, with its backdrop of the Alps and lined with luxurious villian and colorful towns like Bellagio, is stunning. Explore Lake Garda, Italy's largest lake, offering a mix of family-friendly attractions, historic sites like Scaligero Castle, and towns including Sirmione and Riva del Garda.
- **Local Cuisine**: The cuisine of the lakes region focuses on fish from the lakes, polenta, and hearty meats. Try 'missultin', sun-dried fish served with polenta. Lake Garda is known for its olive oil and citrus fruits, so don't miss dishes featuring these local products.

Outdoor Activities

Lombardy offers plenty of outdoor activities. The Alps and the Prealps are great for skiing, trekking, and mountaineering, while the lakes are perfect for sailing, windsurfing, and canoeing.

Transportation

Milan has an efficient public transportation network, including trams, buses, and metro. The lakes region is best explored by car or by ferry services that connect the main towns.

Practical Information

Milan is known for its stylish residents, so pack accordingly. Service charges are usually included in restaurants. Lombardy experiences hot summers and cold, foggy winters. The region can be visited year-round, but spring and fall are ideal for milder weather.

Sample Itinerary

Day 1-3: Discover Milan's artistic and architectural highlights, including the Duomo, Castello Sforzesco, and Santa Maria delle Grazie. Experience Milan's vibrant nightlife in the Navigli District.

Day 4-6: Visit Lake Como, explore the towns of Como and Bellagio, enjoy a boat ride on the lake, and visit the luxurious villas.

Day 7-9: Head to Lake Garda, visit the historical sites, enjoy water sports, and explore the picturesque towns around the lake.

Lombardy, with its blend of cosmopolitan allure and natural charm, offers a delightful exploration of Italy's many faces.

Insider's Extras: Lombardy - Milan and the Lakes

- Milan is Italy's fashion and financial hub, but it's also home to the world's largest collection of Leonardo da Vinci's works.
- Lake Como, one of the Italian Lakes in Lombardy, is known for its celebrity residents.
- Lombardy has more UNESCO World Heritage Sites than any other region in Italy.

Experience the magnificence of the Milan Cathedral, an impressive architectural landmark that leaves visitors in awe.

CHAPTER 7
VENETO - VENICE AND VERONA

Welcome to Veneto, a region steeped in history, culture, and natural beauty. Known for its enchanting cities of Venice and Verona, Veneto offers an immersive journey through charming waterways, stunning architecture, Shakespearean romance, and delicious culinary delights. From the misty lagoon landscapes of Venice to the romantic allure of Verona, Veneto weaves a spell that enchants all who visit.

History

The region of Veneto has been shaped by a rich tapestry of influences over the centuries. Once a thriving hub of the Venetian Republic, the region boasts a history that stretches back to the Roman times and is imbued with periods of foreign rule, including the Byzantine and Austrian empires. This rich history has left a profound influence on the architecture, culture, and traditions of the region.

Cultural Highlights

Veneto is rich in culture and tradition. Its legacy includes the bewitching canals of Venice, the lyrical drama of Verona's Arena opera, the vibrant Carnevale, and the historical regattas. Veneto has also made significant contributions to the world of art, with masters like Titian, Canaletto, and Veronese hailing from this region.

Major Cities and Attractions

Venice

- **Sights**: Venice, the 'floating city', is a marvel of architectural and engineering feats. The city's heart is the Piazza San Marco, home to the stunning St. Mark's Basilica, with its gilded mosaics, and the Doge's Palace, a gothic masterpiece. Don't miss the panoramic view from the Campanile, the city's tallest tower.

    Explore the Grand Canal on a traditional gondola, passing by magnificent palaces and under the Rialto Bridge. Visit the islands of Murano, known for its glass-making tradition; Burano, with its colourful fishermen's houses; and Torcello, home to Venice's first cathedral.

- **Local Cuisine**: Venetian cuisine reflects its lagoon environment. Sample 'sarde in saor' (sweet and sour sardines), 'bigoli in salsa' (whole wheat pasta in an anchovy and onion sauce), and 'risi e bisi' (rice and peas). Seafood lovers should try 'fritto misto' (mixed fried seafood). For dessert, 'tiramisu', a coffee-soaked sponge cake layered with mascarpone cream, is a must-try.

Verona

- **Sights**: Verona, known as the 'city of love' because of Shakespeare's Romeo and Juliet, is a UNESCO World Heritage site. Visit Juliet's House, with the famous balcony, and Romeo's House. The Verona Arena, a Roman amphitheater still in use for spectacular operas, is a must-see.

  Explore the medieval Castelvecchio and its museum, and enjoy views of the city from Torre dei Lamberti. Don't miss the Basilica of San Zeno Maggiore, one of the most important Romanesque buildings in Italy.

- **Local Cuisine**: Veronese cuisine is hearty and varied. Try 'risotto all'Amarone' (risotto cooked with Amarone wine), 'pasta e fasoi' (pasta and bean soup), and 'pastissada de caval' (horse meat stew). For dessert, enjoy 'pandoro', a sweet golden bread originated in Verona.

Outdoor Activities

Veneto offers ample opportunities for outdoor activities. Enjoy boating and rowing in the Venetian lagoon, cycling in the Lessinia Natural Park, or skiing in the Dolomites.

Transportation

Venice is best explored on foot or by water buses (vaporetti). Trains connect Venice with Verona and other cities. Verona is a walkable city, with efficient bus services.

Practical Information

Venetians appreciate a respectful attitude towards their city. Be aware of high-water events (aqua alta) in

Venice. Veneto's climate ranges from Mediterranean on the coast to continental in the hinterland, and it can be visited year-round.

Sample Itinerary

Day 1-3: Explore the artistic and architectural treasures of Venice, including St. Mark's Basilica, the Doge's Palace, and the Rialto Bridge. Take a gondola ride on the Grand Canal.

Day 4: Visit the Venetian islands of Murano, Burano, and Torcello.

Day 5-7: Discover Verona's charm, visit Juliet's House and the Verona Arena, and explore local museums and churches.

Veneto, with its unique blend of history, romance, and natural beauty, offers a uniquely enriching Italian experience.

Insider's Extras: Veneto - The Romance of Venice and Verona

- Venice is built on over 100 small islands and is known for its canals instead of roads.
- The Verona Arena, a well-preserved Roman amphitheater, still hosts operas during the summer.
- The traditional Venetian boat known as a gondola is made up of 280 pieces, each symbolizing a different aspect of Venice.

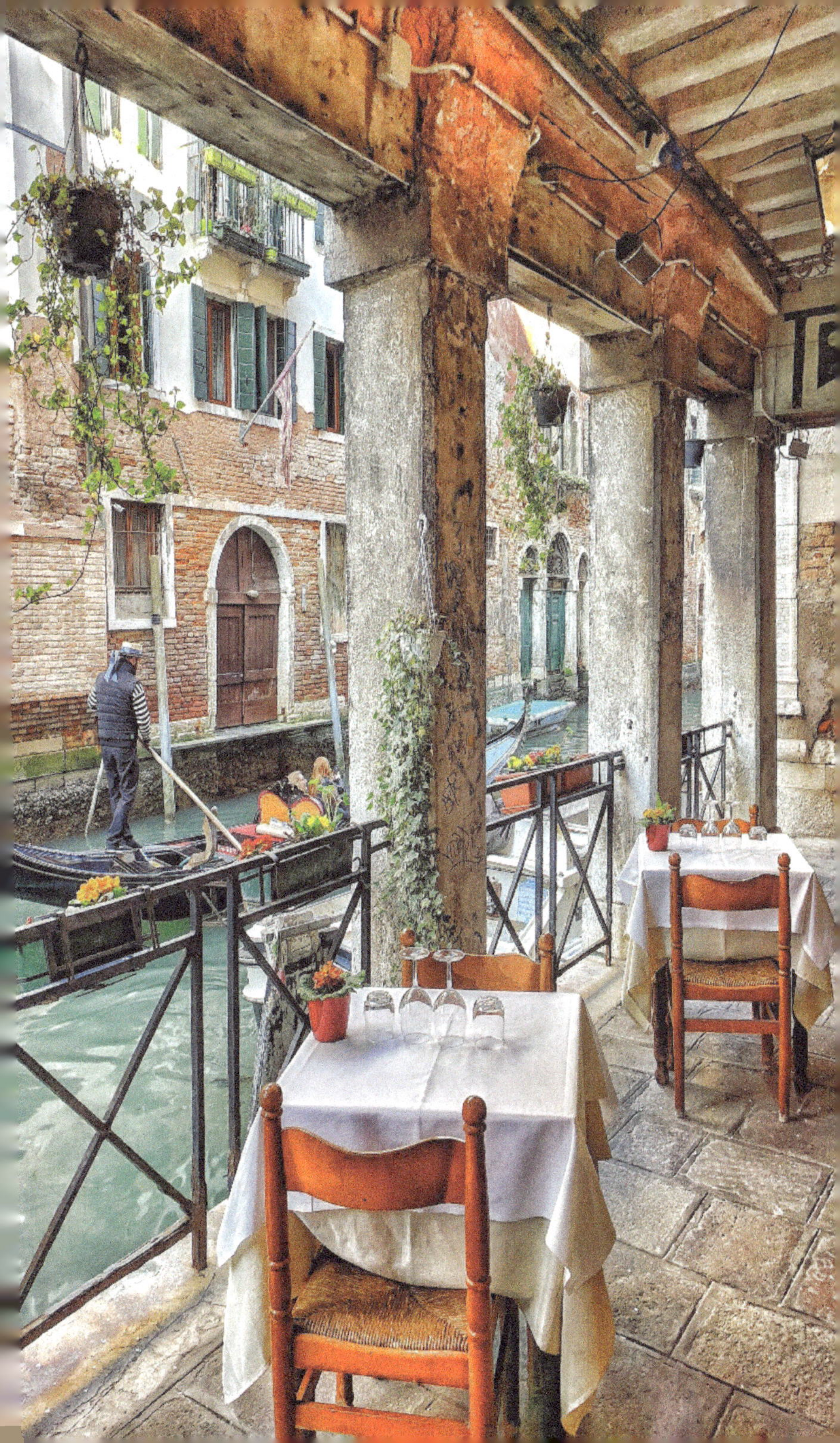

CHAPTER 8
LAZIO - ROME: THE ETERNAL CITY

Welcome to Rome, the heart of Italy and once the center of the ancient world. Known as the Eternal City, Rome carries the weight of history with a mix of grandeur and charm. From ancient ruins and Renaissance masterpieces to delectable cuisine and vibrant streets, Rome is an unforgettable tapestry of experiences.

History

Rome's history spans over two millennia. As the capital of the Roman Empire, the city played a crucial role in shaping Western culture and society. Over the centuries, Rome has undergone various transformations, from the seat of the Papacy to the capital of unified Italy, each phase leaving indelible marks on the city.

Cultural Highlights

Rome's cultural spectrum is vast and varied. It ranges from ancient Roman structures and early Christian sites to Renaissance artworks and Baroque architecture. Rome is also a thriving hub of Italian cinema, fashion, and music, with events like the Rome Film Fest and the Rome Jazz Festival attracting global artists.

Major Attractions

Rome

- **Sights**: Start with the historic heart of Rome, the Colosseum, an architectural marvel and a symbol of the Roman Empire's grandeur. Nearby, visit the Roman Forum and the Palatine Hill, once the epicenter of political, social, and religious activities in Rome.

    Head to the Vatican City to visit St. Peter's Basilica, one of the world's largest churches, and the Vatican Museums, home to an unparalleled collection of art, including the Sistine Chapel with Michelangelo's iconic frescoes.

    Explore the picturesque district of Trastevere, with its narrow cobblestone streets, charming squares, and lively atmosphere. Visit the Pantheon, a beautifully preserved temple dedicated to all the gods of Rome. Don't miss the Trevi Fountain, where you can follow the tradition of throwing a coin to ensure your return to Rome.

- **Local Cuisine**: Roman cuisine is characterized by its simplicity and flavor. Savor 'carbonara' (pasta with egg, cheese, pancetta, and pepper), 'cacio e pepe' (pasta with pecorino cheese and black pepper), and 'amatriciana' (pasta with tomato, pecorino, and guanciale). Enjoy 'carciofi alla Romana' (Roman-style artichokes) and 'supplì' (fried rice balls with mozzarella and ragù). Don't forget to try 'gelato' for dessert.

Outdoor Activities

Rome offers various outdoor activities. Enjoy a walk or a picnic in the Villa Borghese gardens. You can also rent a bike and explore the Appian Way, one of the oldest Roman roads.

Transportation

Rome has a comprehensive public transportation network, including buses, trams, and metro. However, the city is best explored on foot to appreciate its architectural and historical treasures.

Practical Information

When visiting religious sites in Rome, be sure to dress modestly. Rome can be very hot in summer and cool and wet in winter. The city is a year-round destination, but spring and autumn offer the most pleasant weather.

Sample Itinerary

Day 1-2: Visit the Colosseum, Roman Forum, and Palatine Hill. Explore the Pantheon and Trevi Fountain.

Day 3-4: Spend a day in the Vatican City visiting St. Peter's Basilica and the Vatican Museums. Take a walk in Trastevere.

Day 5: Relax in the Villa Borghese gardens or take a bike ride along the Appian Way.

Rome, with its blend of history, art, cuisine, and lively ambiance, offers an enduring charm that captivates all who visit.

Insider's Extras: Lazio - Rome: The Eternal City

- Rome is known as the "Eternal City" because ancient Romans believed that no matter what happened to the world, Rome would go on forever.
- The Vatican City, an independent city-state enclaved within Rome, is the smallest internationally recognized independent state in the world by both area and population.
- There's a city law that forbids anyone to die in the Colosseum.

Immerse yourself in the enchanting atmosphere of the Trevi Fountain, a captivating symbol of beauty and wishes in the heart of Rome.

CHAPTER 9
CAMPANIA - NAPLES, POMPEII, AND THE AMALFI COAST

Campania, a region of southern Italy, is a place of striking contrasts and incredible beauty. From the bustling, vibrant streets of Naples, the quiet, haunting ruins of Pompeii, to the breathtaking views along the Amalfi Coast, Campania is a region that truly embodies the diverse charm of Italy.

History

The history of Campania is a rich tapestry of cultures and civilizations. Founded by the Greeks and later expanded by the Romans, Naples is one of the oldest continuously inhabited cities in the world. The area is also famous for the ancient city of Pompeii, tragically preserved by the eruption of Mount Vesuvius in 79 AD.

Cultural Highlights

Campania is a region of rich cultural traditions, with Naples at its heart. Known for its music, theater, and visual art, Naples has made significant contributions to Italian and European culture.

Major Attractions

Naples

- **Sights**: Begin your journey at the heart of Naples, the historic center, a UNESCO World Heritage Site, with its narrow streets, ancient churches, and bustling piazzas. Visit Naples Cathedral, the Royal Palace, and the Castel Nuovo, an imposing medieval castle.

    The National Archaeological Museum is a must-visit with its extensive collection of Greek and Roman artifacts. Explore the bustling Pignasecca Market, a sensory delight of food, colors, and people. And for a touch of the macabre, venture into the ancient Catacombs of San Gennaro.

- **Local Cuisine**: Naples is the birthplace of pizza, so trying a true Neapolitan pizza is a must. Other local specialties include 'Spaghetti alle Vongole' (spaghetti with clams), 'Ragù Napoletano' (Neapolitan meat sauce), and 'Mozzarella in Carrozza' (deep-fried mozzarella sandwiches). Save room for dessert - Naples is famous for its sweet treats like 'Sfogliatella' (lobster tail pastry) and 'Baba' (rum-soaked cake).

Pompeii

- **Sights**: The archaeological site of Pompeii is a powerful reminder of the destructive power of nature. Walk the ancient streets, see the ruins of homes, shops, and public buildings, and get a sense of life in a Roman city.

Amalfi Coast

- **Sights**: The stunning Amalfi Coast, with its steep cliffs, blue waters, and colorful villages, is a UNESCO World Heritage site. Visit the charming town of Positano, take a stroll in the town of Amalfi and visit its impressive cathedral. Don't forget to visit Ravello with its beautiful villas and gardens.
- **Local Cuisine**: The Amalfi Coast is known for its fresh seafood and citrus fruits. Enjoy 'Scialatielli ai Frutti di Mare' (seafood pasta), and sip on 'Limoncello', a sweet lemon liqueur. Try 'Delizia al Limone', a soft sponge cake filled with lemon cream.

Outdoor Activities

Hiking is a popular activity in Campania, with numerous trails along the Amalfi Coast offering stunning views. Water sports such as sailing and scuba diving are also popular.

Transportation

Naples has a well-developed public transportation system, and the Amalfi Coast is well-serviced by local buses and ferries. Cars are not recommended due to narrow roads and limited parking.

Practical Information

The region can get very hot in the summer, with milder temperatures in the spring and fall. Be aware that many businesses and restaurants close in the afternoon for 'riposo,' the Italian version of a siesta.

Day 1: Immersion in Naples History and Culture

- Morning: Begin your day in Naples with a visit to Piazza del Plebiscito, the city's primary square. Here, take in the sights of majestic structures such as the Royal Palace and Basilica of San Francesco di Paola. Enjoy a traditional Italian espresso at a nearby café.

- Afternoon: Head towards the Castel Nuovo, an iconic medieval castle, followed by a stroll to the port for a view of Mount Vesuvius across the bay. For lunch, stop by a local pizzeria to savor a Neapolitan pizza.
- Evening: Explore the vibrant Spaccanapoli, a narrow, bustling street that cuts through the heart of Naples. Don't miss the Naples Cathedral and end your day with a mouth-watering gelato from a local ice cream shop.

Day 2: Further Exploration of Naples

- Morning: Start your day with a visit to Teatro San Carlo, the oldest active public opera house worldwide. From there, explore the Galleria Umberto I, a picturesque public shopping gallery featuring various shops and eateries.
- Afternoon: Take a trip to the Sansevero Chapel Museum, renowned for its incredible sculpture, the "Veiled Christ." Later, walk around Quartieri Spagnoli, a neighborhood known for its narrow lanes and colorful buildings.
- Evening: Savor a seafood dinner at a restaurant in the Santa Lucia district, offering an unforgettable view of the sea. Try the traditional Spaghetti alle Vongole.

Day 3: Delve into Naples' Historical Treasures

- Morning: Begin at the National Archaeological Museum, which boasts an essential collection of Greek and Roman antiquities. Spend ample time exploring the wide array of exhibits.

- Afternoon: Post a leisurely lunch, visit the Catacombs of San Gennaro. This ancient Christian burial site features stunning frescoes from the 2nd to the 5th century AD.
- Evening: Conclude the day with a hearty Neapolitan meal, such as ragù - a slow-cooked meat sauce paired with pasta.

Day 4: A Day Trip to Pompeii

- Morning/Afternoon: Take a full day to visit Pompeii, the ancient Roman city preserved under volcanic ash from Mount Vesuvius's eruption. Explore significant sites like the Forum, the Baths, and the Amphitheatre. Don't miss the Villa of the Mysteries, which contains some of the best-preserved frescoes in the world.
- Evening: Return to Naples and enjoy a relaxed dinner, perhaps trying another local dish like Parmigiana di Melanzane, a baked eggplant dish.

Day 5-7: Amalfi Coast Exploration

- Day 5: Start your journey along the beautiful Amalfi Coast with the town of Positano. Visit the Church of Santa Maria Assunta, stroll down the narrow streets, and enjoy a beach afternoon. Stay overnight in Positano.
- Day 6: On the second day, head to Amalfi. Visit the stunning Amalfi Cathedral, and spend some time learning about the town's maritime history at the Museum of Paper. If time allows, enjoy a boat ride to experience the coast from the water.
- Day 7: On the final day, visit Ravello, known for its stunning villas - Villa Rufolo and Villa Cimbrone, both offering extraordinary views of the coastline. End the trip with a well-deserved delicious Italian

meal overlooking the scenic beauty of the Amalfi Coast.

Campania, with its vibrant cities, historical ruins, and stunning coastlines, offers an unforgettable Italian experience.

Insider's Extras: Campania: Naples and the Amalfi Coast

- **Naples is the birthplace of pizza, and its Neapolitan style of pizza has earned it the UNESCO Intangible Cultural Heritage status.**
- **The Amalfi Coast is known for its production of limoncello liqueur and the area is a known cultivator of lemons known as sfusato amalfitano.**
- **Capri, a popular tourist destination off the coast of Naples, has been a resort since the time of the Roman Republic.**

Capri's azure waters, adorned with a dance of boats, echoing Italy's timeless allure.

CHAPTER 10
LIGURIA - CINQUE TERRE AND PORTOFINO

Liguria, a crescent-shaped region in northwest Italy, is a charming mix of rugged coastline, colorful villages, and stylish seaside resorts. From the UNESCO World Heritage site of Cinque Terre to the exclusive enclave of Portofino, Liguria offers an enchanting blend of natural beauty and Italian dolce vita.

History

Liguria's history dates back to prehistoric times, with the region being inhabited by various tribes and later becoming part of the Roman Empire. Over the centuries, its strategic position and natural harbors have made it a vital maritime and trading center.

Cultural Highlights

Liguria is the birthplace of the famous explorer Christopher Columbus, and its rich cultural heritage is evident in its art, music, and architecture. The region is also known for its traditional festivals, like the Palio Marinaro in Portofino and the Festa della Madonna Bianca in Cinque Terre.

Major Attractions

Cinque Terre

- **Sights**: Cinque Terre, which means "Five Lands", is a string of five fishing villages perched on the rugged Italian Riviera. They include Monterosso al Mare, Vernazza, Corniglia, Manarola, and Riomaggiore. Each village has its unique charm, but they all share steeply terraced cliffs, colorful houses, and stunning sea views.

  A walking trail, Sentiero Azzurro, connects the villages, offering fantastic views and a chance to experience the region's natural beauty.

- **Local Cuisine**: Cinque Terre's cuisine is based on its bountiful sea and fertile land. Enjoy 'focaccia alla Genovese' (Genoese-style flatbread), 'trofie al pesto' (pasta with pesto sauce), and fresh seafood. Don't miss 'Sciacchetrà', a local sweet wine.

Portofino

- **Sights**: Portofino, once a fishing village, is now a famous holiday resort known for its picturesque harbor and historical landmarks like the Church of St. Martin and the Brown Castle. Visit the Portofino Natural Park for panoramic views of the Ligurian Sea.

- **Local Cuisine**: Portofino's cuisine offers a delightful blend of seafood and local produce. Try 'Pansoti' (stuffed pasta) with walnut sauce, 'Buridda' (fish stew), and 'Focaccia di Recco' (cheese-stuffed flatbread). For dessert, indulge in 'Canestrelli', a typical Ligurian cookie.

Outdoor Activities

Liguria offers excellent hiking and swimming opportunities. Diving and sailing are also popular along its coastline. In Cinque Terre, vineyard tours offer a glimpse into the region's wine-making tradition.

Transportation

Cinque Terre is best explored on foot or by train, as cars are restricted in the villages. Portofino can be reached by boat or bus from Santa Margherita Ligure.

Practical Information

Liguria has a Mediterranean climate with mild winters and warm summers. It can get crowded in summer, so spring and fall may offer a more relaxed experience.

Sample Itinerary

Day 1-3: Explore the villages of Cinque Terre and enjoy the local cuisine.

Day 4-5: Relax in Portofino, visit the landmarks, and enjoy water activities.

Liguria, with its stunning landscapes, charming villages, and delectable cuisine, promises a memorable Italian getaway.

Insider's Extras: Liguria: Cinque Terre and Portofino

- The Cinque Terre, made up of five fishing villages, is a UNESCO World Heritage Site known for its terraced agricultural lands.
- Portofino is known for its picturesque harbor and the colorful, half-moon shaped seaside village.

- Pesto, a sauce originating in Genoa, the region's capital, is a staple of Ligurian cuisine.

A boat poised on tranquil waters, set against the vibrant, terraced backdrop of Cinque Terre.

CHAPTER 11
EMILIA-ROMAGNA - BOLOGNA AND MODENA

Emilia-Romagna, a region known for its rich history, iconic architecture, and mouthwatering cuisine, offers a delightful mix of cultural treasures and gastronomic pleasures. From Bologna's medieval charm to Modena's UNESCO-listed city center, this region is a feast for the senses.

History

The history of Emilia-Romagna is a tapestry of powerful civilizations, including the Etruscans, Celts, and Romans. Bologna and Modena, two of its most prominent cities, were important centers of art and learning during the Middle Ages and the Renaissance.

Cultural Highlights

Emilia-Romagna is a region of culture, music, and motors. Bologna is home to the oldest university in the Western world and an impressive lineup of historic theaters. Modena is famous for its connection to luxury car brands like Ferrari and Maserati.

Major Attractions

Bologna

- **Sights**: Bologna's medieval city center is filled with architectural gems. Visit Piazza Maggiore, the city's main square, surrounded by the Basilica of San Petronio, the City Hall Building, and the Fountain of Neptune. The Two Towers, Asinelli and Garisenda, offer panoramic views of the city.

  The University Quarter is teeming with historic buildings and buzzing with student life. Don't miss the Santo Stefano complex, a fascinating group of interconnected religious edifices.

- **Local Cuisine**: Bologna, often called 'La Grassa' or 'The Fat One,' is a food lover's paradise. Try 'Tagliatelle al Ragu' (ribbon pasta with meat sauce), 'Tortellini in Brodo' (stuffed pasta in broth), and 'Mortadella' (Bologna sausage). For dessert, enjoy 'Zuppa Inglese,' a layered custard and sponge cake.

Modena

- **Sights**: Modena's city center, a UNESCO World Heritage site, is home to impressive landmarks like the Modena Cathedral, the Ghirlandina Tower, and the Ducal Palace. The Enzo Ferrari Museum pays homage to the city's motoring heritage.

- **Local Cuisine**: Modena's culinary scene is renowned, with specialties like 'Tortellini' (stuffed pasta), 'Zampone' (stuffed pig's foot), and 'Cotechino' (pork sausage). Don't miss 'Aceto Balsamico Tradizionale di Modena' (traditional balsamic vinegar) and 'Parmigiano-Reggiano' cheese. For dessert, try 'Torta Barozzi,' a chocolate and almond cake.

Outdoor Activities

Emilia-Romagna offers excellent cycling routes and walking trails. The region is also home to several natural parks and reserves.

Transportation

Bologna and Modena have efficient public transportation networks, including buses and trains. Bologna's central location makes it an ideal base for exploring the region.

Practical Information

Emilia-Romagna has a temperate seasonal climate, with warm summers and cool winters. Some restaurants close in August for vacation, so it's good to check in advance.

Sample Itinerary

Day 1-2: Discover Bologna's medieval center and indulge in local cuisine.

Day 3-4: Explore Modena's UNESCO-listed city center and visit the Enzo Ferrari Museum.

Emilia-Romagna, with its captivating cities, impressive heritage, and culinary delights, provides a deep dive into Italy's cultural and gastronomic heart.

Insider Info: Emilia-Romagna: Bologna and Modena

- Bologna is known as "La Dotta, La Grassa, La Rossa," meaning "the educated, the fat, the red." The city is known for its rich food tradition, red rooftops, and the oldest university in the western world.

- Modena is the birthplace of balsamic vinegar and world-renowned car manufacturers Ferrari and Maserati.
- The region is the origin of popular foods like tortellini, lasagna, Parmesan cheese, and mortadella.

Bologna's vibrant food scene, embodied in a bustling tortellini stand, serving tradition with each bite.

CHAPTER 12
PIEDMONT - TURIN AND THE WINE COUNTRY

Nestled in the foothills of the Alps in northwest Italy, Piedmont is a region that seamlessly blends cosmopolitan charm with pastoral beauty. From the grandeur of Turin, the region's capital, to the vineyard-laced hills of the Langhe and Monferrato areas, Piedmont offers a diverse and enriching travel experience.

History

Piedmont's history is steeped in royalty, as it was the birthplace of the House of Savoy, which later became the ruling house of Italy. Turin was the first capital of unified Italy and still houses the residences of the Savoy.

Cultural Highlights

Piedmont is known for its art, architecture, and literature. Turin hosts internationally acclaimed film, art, and music festivals and is home to the National Cinema Museum. The region is also famous for its wine culture, with the Langhe area recognized as a UNESCO World Heritage Site.

Major Attractions

Turin

- **Sights**: Start your journey in Turin with a visit to the Piazza Castello, the city's main square, home to the Palazzo Reale and Palazzo Madama. The Mole Antonelliana, a tower that is now the National Cinema Museum, dominates the city skyline.

  Visit the Museo Egizio, which hosts an extensive collection of Egyptian antiquities. Wander through the Quadrilatero Romano, the city's old Roman district, known for its vibrant nightlife and food scene.

- **Local Cuisine**: Turin's gastronomy is rich and varied. Savor 'Agnolotti' (meat-filled pasta), 'Bagna Cauda' (a warm dip for vegetables), and 'Vitello Tonnato' (veal with tuna sauce). Don't miss 'Gianduja' chocolate and 'Bicerin', a traditional hot drink made of espresso, chocolate, and cream.

Wine Country - Langhe and Monferrato

- **Sights**: The undulating hills of Langhe and Monferrato, dotted with vineyards and castles, are a sight to behold. Visit the town of Alba, known for its truffles and wine. The Castle of Grinzane Cavour, now a wine museum and UNESCO World Heritage Site, offers panoramic views of the region.

- **Local Cuisine**: The Langhe and Monferrato areas are renowned for their culinary delights. Enjoy 'Tajarin' (thin pasta) with truffles, 'Bollito Misto' (mixed boiled meats), and a variety of cheeses. Pair your meals with local wines like Barolo, Barbaresco, and Moscato d'Asti.

Outdoor Activities

Piedmont offers wonderful opportunities for hiking, biking, and skiing. Wine tours and truffle hunting are popular activities in the Langhe and Monferrato areas.

Transportation

Turin has an excellent public transportation network, including trams, buses, and a metro system. The wine country is best explored by car or on organized tours.

Practical Information

Piedmont has a continental climate, with hot summers and cold winters. The Alba White Truffle Festival, held in October-November, is a popular event.

Sample Itinerary

Day 1-2: Explore Turin's architectural gems and in Day 1-2: Discovering Turin's Architectural Gems and Local Cuisine

Start your journey in Turin with a visit to the Mole Antonelliana in the morning, followed by the National Museum of Cinema. After immersing yourself in the city's culture and history, take an afternoon stroll around the Royal Palace and the Cathedral of Saint John the Baptist. As the evening sets in, dine at a local trattoria, where you can indulge in Bagna Cauda, a traditional dish of the region.

On your second day, visit the historic Palazzo Madama in the morning, followed by a walk to the bustling Piazza Castello. In the afternoon, head to the Automobile Museum and explore the evolution of Italy's car industry. Later, take a peaceful stroll along the scenic Po River and visit Valentino Park. Round off your day with a delicious dinner at an osteria, where you can sample regional cheeses paired with Barolo, a renowned Piedmontese red wine.

Day 3-5: Journey to the Vineyard-laced Landscapes of Langhe and Monferrato

On the third day, head to Alba in the Langhe region. Known for its wine production, Alba will offer you an authentic taste of Italy's viticulture. In the afternoon, visit a local vineyard and immerse yourself in a guided tour, tasting local wines such as Barolo and Barbaresco. Finish your day with a dinner at a local restaurant, enjoying traditional dishes like Tajarin pasta.

Day four will bring an exciting truffle hunting tour. In the company of a local guide and trained dogs, delve into the forests to hunt for this gourmet gem. After the thrilling hunt, visit another vineyard for a relaxing wine tasting session. Spend your evening enjoying the culinary delights of Alba.

On the final day, feel free to explore Langhe and Monferrato at your own pace. This could include additional vineyard visits, exploring other local towns, or simply taking time to relax and soak in the beautiful scenery. This flexible day allows you to tailor your experience to your preferences and interests.

Insider's Extras: Piedmont: Turin and the Wine Country

- Turin, the first capital of Italy, is home to the iconic Shroud of Turin and FIAT automobile company.
- Piedmont is a paradise for wine lovers and is famous for its Barolo and Barbaresco wines.
- The region is also famous for white truffles, especially in the city of Alba, where one of the world's most important truffle fairs takes place annually.

Turin basking in daylight: a cityscape that exudes elegance, history, and an enduring sense of charm.

CHAPTER 13
SICILY - PALERMO AND THE ANCIENT RUINS

Sicily, the largest island in the Mediterranean Sea, is a fascinating blend of cultures, histories, and landscapes. From the vibrant city of Palermo to the ancient ruins scattered across the island, Sicily promises a journey of discovery and delight.

History

Sicily has been at the crossroads of civilizations for thousands of years, from the ancient Greeks and Romans to the Arabs, Normans, and Spaniards. Each has left an indelible mark on the island's culture, architecture, and cuisine.

Cultural Highlights

Sicily is home to several UNESCO World Heritage Sites and is renowned for its music, literature, and festivals. The island's folk traditions, puppet theaters, and vibrant festivals, such as Palermo's Festino di Santa Rosalia, offer a unique cultural experience.

Major Attractions

Palermo

- **Sights**: Palermo, Sicily's capital, is a city of contrasts, where grand palaces and churches stand next to bustling markets. Visit the Norman Palace and the Palatine Chapel, the Teatro Massimo, and the Catacombs of the Capuchins. Wander through the historic districts of La Kalsa and Il Capo, and explore the vibrant Ballarò and Vucciria markets.

- **Local Cuisine**: Palermo's cuisine reflects its multicultural history. Try 'Arancini' (stuffed rice balls), 'Panelle' (chickpea fritters), and 'Caponata' (eggplant stew). For dessert, savor 'Cannoli' (tube-shaped shells of fried pastry dough filled with sweet, creamy ricotta) and 'Cassata Siciliana' (ricotta cake).

Ancient Ruins

- **Sights**: Sicily boasts some of the best-preserved ancient Greek ruins outside of Greece. The Valley of the Temples in Agrigento and the archaeological sites of Segesta and Selinunte are must-visits. The Roman Villa del Casale in Piazza Armerina, with its stunning mosaics, is another highlight.

- **Local Cuisine**: Sicily's ancient sites are surrounded by fertile lands that produce excellent wines, olive oils, and citrus fruits. Enjoy regional specialties like 'Couscous Trapanese' (seafood couscous) and 'Pasta alla Norma' (pasta with tomatoes, eggplant, and ricotta salata). Taste 'Nero d'Avola', Sicily's flagship red wine.

Outdoor Activities

Sicily offers a range of outdoor activities, from hiking on Mount Etna, Europe's highest active volcano, to swimming in the turquoise waters of the Aeolian Islands. The island's natural parks and reserves are perfect for bird watching and nature walks.

Transportation

Palermo has an extensive bus network. To reach the ancient ruins, you can rent a car or join a guided tour.

Practical Information

Sicily has a Mediterranean climate, with hot, dry summers and mild, wet winters. The island can get crowded in summer, so spring and fall are ideal for a more relaxed visit.

Sample Itinerary

Itinerary 1: Palermo and Surroundings

Day 1-2: Explore Palermo's Historic Center and Food Markets

- Day 1:
    - Morning: Start with a visit to the grandiose Palermo Cathedral, a blend of various architectural styles. Then, head to the Norman Palace, home to the Palatine Chapel.
    - Afternoon: Stroll down the bustling Via Maqueda, and explore the Quattro Canti, an iconic baroque square. Visit the Church of Saint Joseph of the Theatines.
    - Evening: Enjoy traditional Sicilian dishes like Caponata or Pasta alla Norma at a local Trattoria.

Sicily - Palermo and the Ancient Ruins

- Day 2:
    - Morning: Begin the day at the Ballarò Market, a colorful and lively food market where you can sample fresh local produce, cheeses, and street food.
    - Afternoon: Visit the Teatro Massimo, Italy's largest opera house. Then, explore the Capuchin Catacombs for an intriguing look into Palermo's history.
    - Evening: Relish Sicilian seafood at a local Osteria.

Day 3-5: Visit the Ancient Ruins

- Day 3: Take a day trip to the ancient Greek site of Segesta. Explore the well-preserved Doric temple and the ancient theater.
- Day 4: Head towards Selinunte, home to the largest archaeological park in Europe, featuring ruins of ancient Greek temples.
- Day 5: Visit Agrigento's Valley of the Temples, an impressive collection of Greek temples. Return to Palermo for the night.
- Itinerary 2: Catania and Surroundings
- Day 1-2: Explore Catania's Historic Center and Food Markets

- Day 1:
    - Morning: Start at the Piazza Duomo, Catania's main square, and visit the Cathedral of Sant'Agata. Take a walk to Ursino Castle, a historic fortress now serving as a museum.
    - Afternoon: Walk along Via Etnea, the city's main shopping street. Visit the Roman Theater and the Odeon.

- Evening: Dine at a local restaurant and try the famous Pasta alla Norma.
- Day 2:
  - Morning: Visit La Pescheria, the vibrant fish market. Sample Sicilian cheeses and street food like Arancini.
  - Afternoon: Take a trip to the nearby town of Aci Castello and visit its Norman Castle.
  - Evening: Enjoy Sicilian seafood at a seafront restaurant.

Day 3-5: Explore the Historic Sites

- Day 3: Visit Piazza Armerina and the Villa Romana del Casale, a Roman villa known for its well-preserved mosaics.
- Day 4: Take a day trip to Syracuse, explore the Archaeological Park of Neapolis, featuring the Greek Theatre, the Roman Amphitheatre, and the Ear of Dionysius.
- Day 5: Visit Taormina, explore its Greek Theatre, and enjoy the stunning views of Mount Etna and the sea. Return to Catania for the night.

Each itinerary offers a unique perspective on Sicily's rich history, vibrant culture, and delicious food. You can mix and match these itineraries or modify them according to your preferences.

Insider's Extras: Sicily: Palermo and the Ancient Ruins

- Sicily is home to Mount Etna, the tallest active volcano in Europe.

- The Valley of the Temples, near Agrigento, is one of the best-preserved examples of Greek Doric architecture.
- Sicily has been ruled by numerous nations over the centuries, each leaving its mark, from Arab-influenced architecture to Greek temples and Roman amphitheaters.

*Palermo's pulsating lifeblood: its vibrant
streets teeming with energy, history, and the unceasing
rhythm of Sicilian life.*

CHAPTER 14
PUGLIA - BARI AND THE ADRIATIC COAST

Puglia, or Apulia, the heel of Italy's boot, is a sun-drenched region known for its whitewashed towns, crystal-clear Adriatic Sea, and acres of olive groves. Bari, the capital, exudes old-world charm, while the Adriatic Coast is a haven for beach lovers.

History

Puglia's strategic location has made it a crossroads of civilizations, from the ancient Greeks and Romans to the Normans, Swabians, and Bourbons. Each has left their mark, contributing to the region's rich cultural and architectural tapestry.

Cultural Highlights

Puglia is known for its folk music, traditional dance (the Pizzica), and unique festivals. The region is home to numerous castles, including the Castel del Monte, a UNESCO World Heritage site.

Major Attractions

Bari

- **Sights**: Begin your exploration in Bari Vecchia, the city's old town, with its winding streets, stunning Basilica di San Nicola, and impressive Bari Castle. Visit the bustling fish market at the Old Port and the elegant boulevards of the Murattiano district.

- **Local Cuisine**: Bari's culinary scene is marked by fresh seafood and simple, rustic dishes. Savor 'Orecchiette con Cime di Rapa' (ear-shaped pasta with turnip greens), 'Friselle' (dried bread topped with tomatoes and olive oil), and 'Tiella Barese' (a baked dish with rice, potatoes, and mussels). For dessert, try 'Cartellate', honey-infused pastries.

Adriatic Coast

- **Sights**: The Adriatic Coast boasts pristine beaches and charming towns. Visit Polignano a Mare, famous for its cliffside views, and Trani, with its stunning cathedral by the sea. Don't miss the UNESCO-listed Alberobello, known for its traditional Trulli houses, and the whitewashed city of Ostuni.

- **Local Cuisine**: The Adriatic Coast offers fresh seafood and local produce. Enjoy 'Cozze Ripiene' (stuffed mussels), 'Risotto ai Frutti di Mare' (seafood risotto), and 'Pasticciotto' (cream-filled pastry). Taste the region's crisp white wines, like Verdeca and Bombino Bianco.

Outdoor Activities

Puglia offers excellent hiking, cycling, and water sports opportunities. The region is also home to several nature reserves and national parks.

Transportation

Bari has an efficient public transportation system, including buses and a metro. Exploring the Adriatic Coast is best done by car or on organized tours.

Practical Information

Puglia has a Mediterranean climate, with hot, dry summers and mild winters. Many businesses close for a few hours in the afternoon for siesta, particularly in smaller towns.

Sample Itinerary

Day 1-2: Explore Bari's old town and savor local cuisine.

Day 3-5: Discover the charming towns and beautiful beaches along the Adriatic Coast.

Puglia, with its charming cities, stunning coastline, and delectable cuisine, is a region that offers an authentic and relaxing Italian experience.

Insider Info: Puglia - Bari and the Adriatic Coast

- The Trulli of Alberobello, unique limestone dwellings in Puglia, are a UNESCO World Heritage Site.
- Puglia produces over a third of Italy's olive oil.
- The town of Polignano a Mare, located on the Adriatic Sea, is famous for the Red Bull Cliff Diving competition.

The trulli of Alberobello, Puglia - whimsical stone dwellings that personify the charm and uniqueness of Italy's built heritage.

CHAPTER 15

THE GRAPE ESCAPE: WINES OF ITALY AND THEIR PAIRINGS

Italy is synonymous with wine. From the sun-drenched slopes of Sicily to the misty vineyards of Piedmont, every region boasts its own unique variety of grapes, methods of production, and, of course, enchanting wines. From robust reds to crisp whites and effervescent sparklings, Italian wines offer a delightful array of tastes and aromas to explore and savor.

In this chapter, we journey through the stunning wine regions of Italy, showcasing the signature wines from each region, complete with suggested food pairings to enhance your culinary experiences. Whether you're a novice wine enthusiast or a seasoned oenophile, this guide will equip you with the knowledge to fully appreciate the wonderful world of Italian wines.

Discover how the robust Chianti from Tuscany enhances the flavors of a hearty pasta dish, how the crisp Vermentino from Liguria pairs beautifully with fresh seafood, or how the rich and full-bodied Barolo from Piedmont is the perfect accompaniment to red meat and mature cheeses.

As you travel through Italy, let each glass of wine you enjoy not only quench your thirst but also deepen your understanding and appreciation of the region's culture, tradition, and way of life. Because in Italy, wine is more than just a beverage — it's a celebration of life, a tribute to nature, and an embodiment of the timeless Italian spirit. Let's embark on this unforgettable 'Grape Escape' through the vineyards of Italy. Salute!

Tuscany: Florence and Siena

- **Chianti**: This robust red wine pairs well with pasta dishes, grilled meat, and mature cheeses.

- **Brunello di Montalcino**: A rich and full-bodied red wine, best enjoyed with game, red meat, and aged cheese.

- **Vernaccia di San Gimignano**: A crisp white wine, it's perfect with seafood, light appetizers, and poultry.

Lombardy: Milan and the Lakes

- **Franciacorta**: A sparkling white wine, great as an aperitif, with seafood, or light appetizers.

- **Oltrepo Pavese**: A versatile wine that comes in red, white, and sparkling varieties. Pairs well with a variety of dishes from grilled meat to fish.

- **Sforzato di Valtellina**: A strong, rich red wine, perfect with game and mature cheeses.

Veneto: The Romance of Venice and Verona

- **Amarone della Valpolicella**: A rich, full-bodied red wine that pairs well with game, mature cheeses, and hearty stews.

- **Prosecco**: This popular sparkling wine is a great aperitif and pairs well with light appetizers and seafood.
- **Soave**: A dry white wine that's excellent with fish, white meat, and risotto.

Lazio - Rome: The Eternal City

- **Frascati**: A light and fruity white wine, best enjoyed with fish, white meat, or Roman-style artichokes.
- **Est! Est!! Est!!! di Montefiascone**: A historic white wine, great with fish and light appetizers.
- **Cesanese del Piglio**: A full-bodied red that pairs well with meat dishes and mature cheeses.

Campania: Naples and the Amalfi Coast

- **Aglianico (Taurasi)**: A robust red wine, perfect with red meat, game, and hearty stews.
- **Fiano di Avellino**: A fragrant and full-bodied white wine, great with seafood, poultry, and risotto.
- **Falanghina**: A crisp and aromatic white that pairs well with seafood, especially shellfish.

Liguria: Cinque Terre and Portofino

- **Cinque Terre**: A dry white wine that pairs excellently with seafood.
- **Rossese di Dolceacqua**: A light red wine that matches well with red meat and mature cheeses.
- **Vermentino**: An aromatic white that goes well with fish, shellfish, and light appetizers.

Emilia-Romagna: Bologna and Modena

- **Lambrusco**: A fizzy red wine, best enjoyed with charcuterie, pasta dishes, and cheeses.
- **Albana di Romagna**: A versatile wine available in dry, sweet, and passito versions. Pairs well with a variety of dishes from seafood to dessert.
- **Pignoletto**: A sparkling white, excellent as an aperitif, with seafood, or light appetizers.

Piedmont: Turin and the Wine Country

- **Barolo**: Known as "the king of wines", this full-bodied red pairs well with red meat, game, and mature cheeses.
- **Barbaresco**: A robust and elegant red that goes well with hearty meat dishes and mature cheeses.
- **Moscato d'Asti**: A sweet and lightly sparkling white wine, perfect as a dessert wine.

Sicily: Palermo and the Ancient Ruins

- **Nero d'Avola**: Sicily's most important red wine, great with red meat, game, and mature cheeses.
- **Marsala**: A fortified wine that can be dry or sweet. Dry versions pair well with cheese, while sweet versions are perfect for desserts.
- **Etna Bianco**: A white wine produced in the volcanic soils of Mount Etna, pairs well with seafood and fish dishes.

Puglia: Bari and the Adriatic Coast

- **Primitivo**: A full-bodied red wine, great with red meat, hearty stews, and mature cheeses.

- **Negroamaro**: A robust and spicy red that pairs well with game, grilled meat, and strong cheeses.
- **Verdeca**: A fruity and fresh white wine that goes well with fish and light appetizers.

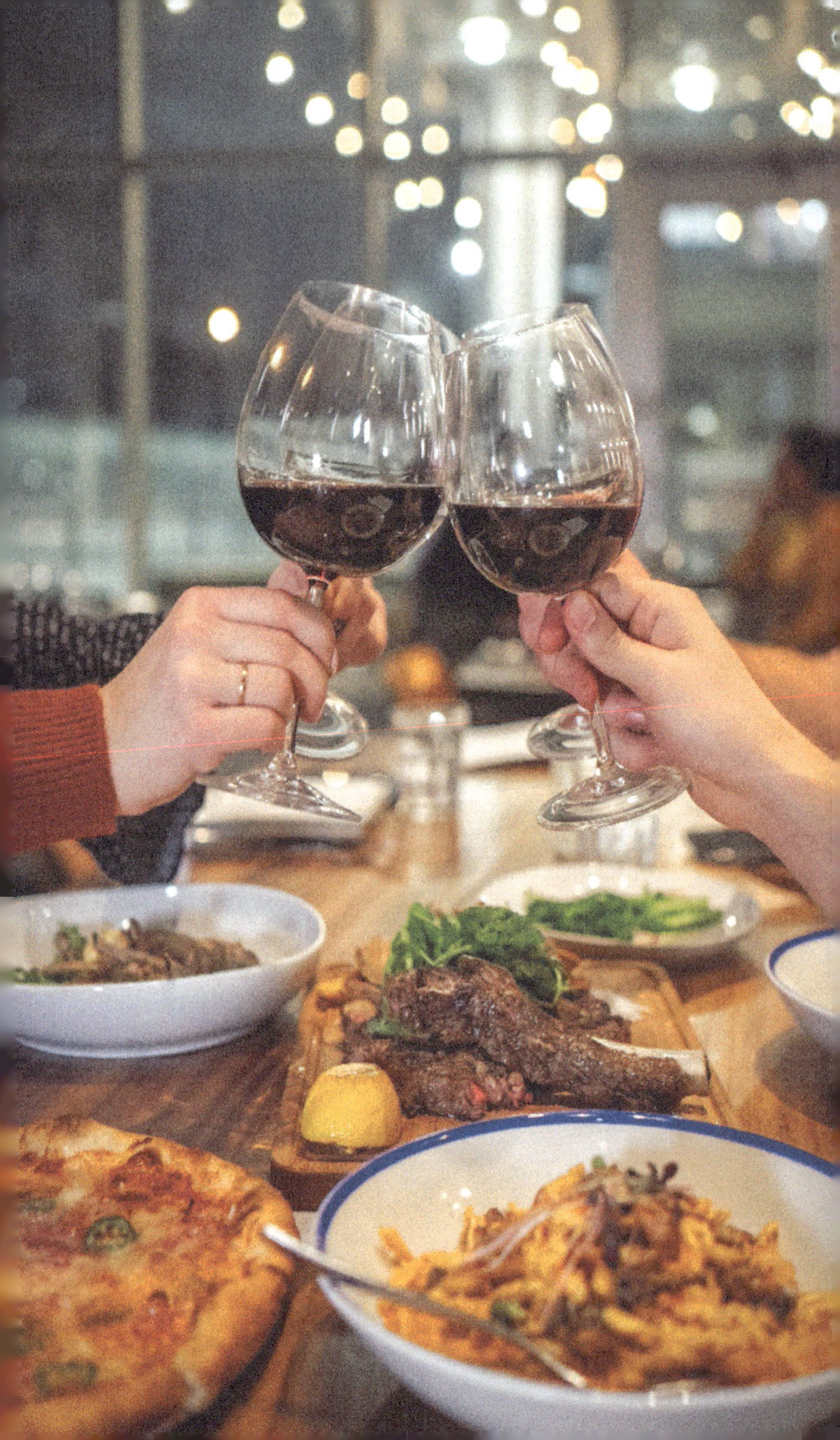

CHAPTER 16
BUILDING YOUR ITINERARY - TAILORING YOUR ITALIAN ADVENTURE

Designing an itinerary can be a daunting task. With so much to see and do, it's easy to feel overwhelmed. However, the key to a successful journey is balance. A well-crafted itinerary will allow you to explore Italy's marvels at your own pace, providing a mix of major landmarks, hidden gems, gastronomic experiences, and relaxation time. Here's how to build your perfect Italian adventure.

Step 1: Define Your Travel Style

Before you start planning, identify what kind of traveler you are. Are you a history buff, a foodie, an outdoor adventurer, or a relaxation seeker? Maybe you're a blend of all. By knowing your travel style, you can tailor your itinerary to your interests.

Step 2: Consider the Duration of Your Trip

The length of your trip will greatly influence your itinerary. If you're visiting for a week, you might want to focus on one or two regions. For a longer stay, you could explore multiple areas or dive deeper into your chosen locales.

Step 3: Choose Your Destinations

From the regions outlined in this book, choose the ones that speak most to your interests. Each offers its unique blend of culture, history, gastronomy, and natural beauty.

Step 4: Plot Your Route

Start by placing your chosen destinations on a map. Then connect the dots in a logical, efficient order. Consider travel times and modes of transportation between locations.

Step 5: Delve into Each Destination

Now it's time to detail what you'll do in each place. This is where the earlier chapters of this book come in handy. Consider the major attractions, outdoor activities, food and drink experiences, and local events in each location.

Step 6: Balance Your Days

Avoid cramming too much into a single day. Striking a balance between sightseeing, leisure, and travel time will ensure a more enjoyable trip. Allow time for spontaneous discoveries – they often become the highlights of your journey!

Step 7: Book in Advance

Once you've finalized your itinerary, book your accommodation, transportation, and any special activities or visits. Some attractions, particularly in high season, require advance booking.

Step 8: Keep It Flexible

Remember, an itinerary is a guide, not a strict schedule. Be flexible and open to changes. Sometimes, the weather, unexpected closures, or simply a newly discovered spot may alter your plans. And that's perfectly okay!

Building your itinerary is the first exciting step in your Italian adventure. It gives you the framework to immerse in Italy's rich culture, breathtaking landscapes, and unforgettable flavors at your own pace. So, dive into the planning process with an open mind and an eager heart, and prepare for an incredible journey. Buon viaggio!

CHAPTER 17
TRAVEL ETIQUETTE - NAVIGATING ITALY WITH GRACE AND RESPECT

Traveling is not just about exploring new places, tasting different foods, or capturing beautiful landscapes. It's also about embracing local customs, understanding cultural nuances, and respecting social norms. As you embark on your Italian adventure, it's essential to navigate Italy with grace and respect. Here are some etiquette tips to help you do just that.

1. Greetings and Politeness

Italians value politeness and formalities. When meeting people, a simple 'Buongiorno' (good morning) or 'Buonasera' (good evening) goes a long way. Always say 'Per favore' (please) when asking for something and 'Grazie' (thank you) to show appreciation.

2. Dress Code

Italians take pride in their appearance, and a sense of style is important. Dress neatly when you're out, and avoid wearing beachwear in the city. When visiting religious sites, cover your shoulders and knees as a sign of respect.

3. Dining Etiquette

When dining, remember to say 'Buon appetito' before starting your meal. Wait for a toast before drinking and always return the gesture with a 'Salute'. It's customary to finish all the food on your plate. Tipping isn't obligatory, but it's appreciated for good service.

4. Respect the Environment

Italy is home to countless natural and cultural treasures. Respect these by not littering, avoiding touching artworks or monuments, and adhering to guidelines in protected areas.

5. Understand the Concept of 'La Pausa'

In many Italian towns, businesses and shops close for a few hours in the afternoon for 'la pausa', a relaxing break. Be aware of this custom to avoid disappointment.

6. Speak Some Italian

Italians appreciate it when visitors try to speak their language. Even a few basic phrases can enhance your interactions with locals.

7. Respect Privacy

Italians value their privacy. Avoid asking personal questions unless you're well-acquainted with someone. Also, ask for permission before taking photos of people.

8. Queuing

While queuing may seem less structured in Italy than in other countries, it's important to wait your turn patiently, whether it's at the bus stop, in the grocery store, or at popular attractions.

Traveling with etiquette and respect allows you to experience Italy's beauty in the most enriching way possible. It paves the way for deeper connections with locals, enhances your understanding of Italian culture, and leaves a positive impact on the places you visit. So, embrace these etiquette tips as you delve into your Italian adventure, and enjoy the warmth and hospitality that Italy has to offer.

9. Security Tip

Italy is generally a safe country for travelers. However, like any popular tourist destination, beware of pickpockets, particularly in crowded areas. Blend in with the local crowd as much as possible, keep your belongings secure and maintain vigilance in busy tourist spots.

10. Bargaining

While prices in larger stores and restaurants are generally fixed, you can often negotiate at smaller stores, outdoor markets, or with street vendors. Polite haggling over prices is an accepted practice and can help you get a better deal.

Immersed in the vibrant tempo of Verona's downtown, where timeless charm meets the lively buzz of modern Italian life.

CHAPTER 18
USEFUL ITALIAN PHRASES - COMMUNICATING WITH LOCALS

Navigating through Italy becomes much more enjoyable when you can communicate, even just a little, in Italian. The Italian language is full of passion and expressive phrases. While many Italians do speak English, especially in tourist areas, knowing some basic Italian phrases can be greatly appreciated and can also make your travel experience more rewarding.

Here are some essential phrases to help you get by:

Greetings

1. Good morning - Buongiorno
2. Good afternoon/evening - Buonasera
3. Good night - Buonanotte
4. Hello/Hi - Ciao
5. Goodbye - Arrivederci

Politeness

6. Please - Per favore
7. Thank you - Grazie
8. You're welcome - Prego
9. Excuse me - Mi scusi

Getting Around

10. Where is...? - Dov'è...?
11. Left - Sinistra
12. Right - Destra
13. Straight ahead - Dritto
14. Map - Mappa

Dining Out

15. I would like... - Vorrei...
16. Water - Acqua
17. Wine - Vino
18. Check, please - Il conto, per favore
19. Delicious - Delizioso

Emergencies

20. Help - Aiuto
21. I need a doctor - Ho bisogno di un dottore
22. Police - Polizia

Numbers

23. One - Uno
24. Two - Due
25. Three - Tre

26. Four - Quattro

27. Five - Cinque

Making Connections

28. What's your name? - Come ti chiami?

29. My name is... - Mi chiamo...

30. Nice to meet you - Piacere

Shops and Purchasing

31. Shop - Negozio

32. Open - Aperto

33. Closed - Chiuso

34. How much does it cost? - Quanto costa?

35. I'd like to buy... - Vorrei comprare...

36. Do you accept credit cards? - Accettate carte di credito?

37. I'm just looking, thanks - Sto solo guardando, grazie

38. Can I try it on? - Posso provarlo?

39. It's too expensive - È troppo caro

40. Do you have it in a smaller/larger size? - Avete una taglia più piccola/grande?

Insider's Extras

Speak Italian: Italians generally appreciate when tourists make an effort to speak their language. So don't be shy to practice your Italian. Even a few phrases can go a long way in connecting with locals and immersing yourself in Italian culture. Remember, practice makes perfect!

Engage with Locals: The true essence of Italian culture goes beyond sightseeing. Engage with locals at cafes, restaurants, markets, or even in the streets. Speaking a little Italian, showing interest in their culture, and being open to their hospitality can unlock unforgettable experiences and friendships. A smile and 'grazie' (thank you) can go a long way!

Knowing these basic Italian phrases can make your Italian adventure more engaging and enjoyable. Remember, it's not just about the words you say but also the enthusiasm and respect with which you say them. Happy practicing and Buon viaggio!

CHAPTER 19
ITALY UNLEASHED – EMBRACE THE OUTDOORS

Tuscany: Florence and Siena Tuscany, with its rolling hills, olive groves, and vineyards, is perfect for biking. For a picturesque route, cycle through the Val d'Orcia, a UNESCO World Heritage Site. Hikers can explore the rugged Apennine Mountains or the trails on the island of Elba in the Tyrrhenian Sea. If you prefer a more serene experience, drift over the Chianti region in a hot air balloon at dawn and toast the experience with a glass of local wine.

Lombardy: Milan and the Lakes The beautiful lakes of Lombardy, particularly Como and Garda, are a haven for water sports enthusiasts. Enjoy windsurfing, sailing, or paddleboarding on their sparkling waters. The surrounding mountain trails offer excellent opportunities for hiking and biking. In winter, the Alps of Lombardy turn into a snowy playground with skiing and snowboarding at resorts like Livigno or Bormio.

Veneto: Venice and Verona Explore the Venetian lagoon in a different way by kayaking or stand-up paddleboarding through its network of canals. For bird watchers, the lagoon's wetlands are a paradise. In Verona, take advantage of the close proximity to Lake Garda, where you can windsurf, sail, or swim in the crystal-clear water. There are also numerous hiking and biking trails around the lake.

Lazio - Rome: The Eternal City While Rome itself is filled with historic sites, it also offers green spaces like the Villa Borghese gardens, ideal for a bike ride or jog. Outside the city, Lazio's diverse landscapes offer fantastic hiking opportunities. The region has several national parks and reserves, including the Circeo National Park, a hotspot for bird watching and trekking.

Campania: Naples and the Amalfi Coast Campania's azure sea offers excellent opportunities for snorkeling, scuba diving, and boating. Hiking enthusiasts should not miss the Path of the Gods (Sentiero degli Dei) on the Amalfi Coast, with breathtaking views over the Mediterranean. For an adventurous ascent, climb Mount Vesuvius and look into the crater of one of Europe's few active volcanoes.

Liguria: Cinque Terre and Portofino The five villages of the Cinque Terre, perched on the rugged coastline of Liguria, are linked by one of Italy's most famous hiking trails. This coastal path offers stunning views over the Mediterranean. In the glamorous town of Portofino, charter a yacht for the day or join a diving expedition to explore the Portofino Marine Protected Area.

Emilia-Romagna: Bologna and Modena The countryside surrounding Bologna and Modena offers lovely hiking and biking opportunities, with routes through vineyards and along riverbanks. The Apennine Mountains, stretching across the south of Emilia-Romagna, are ideal for hiking in summer and skiing in winter. The region also hosts several marathons and cycling races throughout the year.

Piedmont: Turin and the Wine Country The vineyard-laced hills of the Langhe and Roero regions are perfect for leisurely biking or hiking, with the reward of a wine tasting at the end. In winter, the snow-capped Alps offer excellent skiing and snowboarding, particularly in the Via Lattea (Milky Way) ski area.

Sicily: Palermo and the Ancient Ruins Sicily's diverse landscapes make it an outdoor lover's paradise. Hike up Mount Etna, Europe's largest active volcano, or walk among the ancient Greek temples in the Valley of the Temples. The coastline offers beautiful beaches for swimming and cliffs for diving. You can also explore the region's nature reserves, such as the Zingaro Nature Reserve, with its stunning coastal and mountain trails.

Puglia - Bari and the Adriatic Coast Puglia offers a variety of water sports, thanks to its extensive coastline. Kitesurfing, windsurfing, and sailing are popular activities. You can also rent a bike and cycle through ancient olive groves, stopping to explore historical towns or relax on a sandy beach. For a unique experience, try a guided tour of the region's trulli (traditional dry-stone huts) on horseback.

Embracing the serene splendor of the Dolomites, where Italy's breathtaking natural canvas unveils itself.

CHAPTER 20
LA DOLCE VITA - NIGHTLIFE IN ITALY

Experience Italy's vibrant nightlife, characterized by its unique mix of sophistication, vibrancy, and charm. This chapter offers a glimpse into the after-hours ambiance that each of our highlighted regions presents.

Tuscany: Florence and Siena In Florence, the hip Oltrarno district buzzes with life after sunset. Visit a trendy bar like Negroni or Rex for an aperitivo - a pre-dinner drink accompanied by small bites. For club-goers, spaces around Piazza della Repubblica like Full Up or YAB offer a chance to dance till dawn. In Siena, the intimate city center comes alive at night, with wine lovers congregating at enotecas such as La Prosciutteria or Enoteca I Terzi to sample local varietals.

Lombardy: Milan and the Lakes Milan's nightlife pulsates with energy. The Navigli district, renowned for its canal-side establishments, offers everything from eclectic bars like Mag Cafè to energetic clubs like Alcatraz. For a more laid-back experience, the serene settings of Lake Como and Lake Garda provide opportunities for intimate lakeside dinners, with Villa d'Este and Lido di Bellagio being prime spots on Como.

Veneto: Venice and Verona While Venice may evoke images of moonlit gondola rides, areas like Dorsoduro offer a youthful vibe with lively bacari (wine bars) such as Osteria Al Squero. In Verona, open-air operas at the ancient Roman Arena during summer provide a magical, unforgettable experience.

Lazio - Rome: The Eternal City Rome's nightlife is a mélange of styles. Trastevere, with its cobbled streets, hosts trendy cocktail bars like Freni e Frizioni. The Testaccio district, on the other hand, is home to nightclubs such as Goa Club known for its electronic music scene. Theatre lovers can enjoy world-class operas at the Teatro dell'Opera.

Campania: Naples and the Amalfi Coast In Naples, start your evening with a pizza in the bustling historic center, then move to bars like Bar del Fico for cocktails. On the Amalfi Coast, sophisticated cliffside bars like Franco's Bar in Positano or Terrazza Vittoria in Sorrento serve cocktails with a stunning backdrop of the Mediterranean.

Liguria: Cinque Terre and Portofino Cinque Terre's nightlife, much like its lifestyle, is relaxed. Enjoy the local dessert wine Sciacchetrà at a sea-facing bar like Nessun Dorma in Manarola. In the upscale Portofino, head to Winterose Wine Bar for a late-night glass of wine and live music.

Emilia-Romagna: Bologna and Modena With its sizable student population, Bologna has a youthful nightlife scene. Piazza Verdi and Via Zamboni are filled with lively bars like Barazzo where you can enjoy a spritz. Modena offers a slower pace with traditional osterias serving local wines, like Enoteca Compagnia del Taglio.

Piedmont: Turin and the Wine Country Turin's nightlife is marked by its elegant lounges and jazz clubs. Begin your evening at a rooftop bar like Caffè Elena for views over the city. If you're in the Langhe region, spend your evenings at a local trattoria such as More e Macine, paired with the region's renowned wines.

Sicily: Palermo and the Ancient Ruins Palermo's vibrant street food culture continues into the night at markets like Vucciria or Ballarò. For a different experience, attend a moonlit performance at the ancient Greek theater in Taormina, such as the annual Taormina Arte festival.

Puglia - Bari and the Adriatic Coast Bari's nightlife is laid-back yet delightful. Start with a passeggiata (evening stroll) through the old town before heading to a wine bar like Enoteca Decanter. In summer, the Adriatic Coast's beach clubs like White Beach in Torre Canne turn into lively party venues.

Insider's Extras

Many Italian nightclubs, or 'discoteche,' have a 'selezione all'ingresso,' meaning they screen guests at the entrance based on attire and appearance. To ensure a smooth entry, dress stylishly and adhere to the club's dress code. When in doubt, remember Italians are known for their smart, elegant fashion.

As a reminder, nightlife in Italy typically starts late, with many establishments only getting busy after midnight. Pace yourself, enjoy the slow rhythm of Italian life, and experience the joy of la dolce vita.

Nightlife by the Tevere: Rome's animated night market brimming with life and local charm, set against the serene backdrop of the iconic Tiber River.

CHAPTER 21
UNIQUE ITALIAN EXPERIENCES - BEYOND SIGHTSEEING

Italy is full of unique experiences that allow visitors to immerse themselves in the local culture. Beyond the classic sightseeing activities, here are 20 unique things to try in Italy for a truly authentic experience:

1. **Aperitivo**: This pre-dinner ritual is not just about the drink, but the social atmosphere and complimentary snacks that accompany it. The concept originated in Milan but is popular throughout Italy.

2. **Cooking Class**: Italy is renowned for its cuisine. Join a cooking class to learn how to prepare traditional dishes, such as homemade pasta or pizza.

3. **Opera in Verona**: Experience the beauty of Italian opera in the grand Arena di Verona, a Roman amphitheatre that still hosts performances today.

4. **Truffle Hunting**: Venture into the woods with expert truffle hunters and their trained dogs in regions like Piedmont or Tuscany. Savour the delicacy in a meal afterwards.

5. **Climb an Active Volcano**: For a touch of adventure, hike up active volcanoes such as Mount Etna or Stromboli in Sicily. The views are absolutely worth the effort.

6. **Wine Tasting**: Visit local vineyards in regions such as Tuscany, Piedmont or Veneto. Learn about the winemaking process and savour some of the world's best wines.

7. **Visit a Local Market**: Browse the vibrant stalls at a local market, try regional specialties, buy fresh produce, and soak in the daily life of Italians.

8. **Gondola Ride in Venice**: Despite being a quintessential tourist activity, exploring the Venetian canals by gondola offers a unique perspective of the city.

9. **Attend a Local Festival**: Italy hosts countless festivals throughout the year, celebrating everything from art and music to food and historical events.

10. **Explore Ancient Ruins**: Wander through historical sites like Pompeii, Herculaneum, or the Greek ruins in Sicily to delve into Italy's rich past.

11. **Take a Vespa Tour**: Navigate through narrow streets and picturesque landscapes on a Vespa, a classic Italian mode of transportation.

12. **Visit a Cheese Farm**: Learn how Italian cheeses like Parmesan and Mozzarella are made, and enjoy a tasting session at a local farm.

13. **Stay in an Agriturismo**: Experience rural life by staying in an agriturismo, a farm stay that offers accommodations and fresh, farm-to-table meals.

14. **Coffee Culture**: Italian coffee culture is unique. Try a traditional espresso standing at a bar, just like the locals.

15. **Basilica di San Francesco**: Visit Assisi and the Basilica di San Francesco for a spiritual journey, regardless of your religious beliefs.
16. **Ceramic Shopping in Deruta**: Deruta, a small town in Umbria, is famous for its hand-painted ceramics. Visit local workshops and pick up a unique souvenir.
17. **Take a Hot Air Balloon Ride**: For a bird's eye view of Italy's breathtaking landscapes, take a hot air balloon ride over regions like Tuscany or Umbria.
18. **Ferrari Test Drive**: If you're a car enthusiast, head to Maranello, near Modena, to visit the Ferrari museum and even test drive a Ferrari.
19. **Hiking in the Dolomites**: The Dolomites offer some of the most stunning mountain landscapes in the world. There are trails for all levels of hikers.
20. **Visit an Olive Oil Mill**: Similar to wine, olive oil varies greatly by region. Visit a mill to learn about the production process and taste different varieties.

These experiences will add depth to your Italian adventure, turning it from a sightseeing trip into a rich cultural immersion. Buon viaggio!

CHAPTER 22
ARRIVEDERCI, ITALY - FINAL THOUGHTS

As we draw our journey to a close, we hope you're leaving with a profound appreciation for Italy's grandeur - its stunning landscapes, rich history, artistic heritage, and of course, the unforgettable culinary adventures.

Italy is a country that leaves a mark on its visitors, not just with its world-renowned sights, but through the smaller moments: A leisurely meal shared with loved ones, the discovery of an off-the-beaten-path village, a captivating sunset over rolling vineyards, the first bite of an authentic, wood-fired pizza, or the comforting aroma of a perfectly brewed espresso.

Through this book, we have endeavored to guide you through Italy's most popular regions, each with its unique character and offerings. From the romantic canals of Venice to the bustling streets of Rome, the scenic vineyards of Tuscany to the azure waters of the Amalfi Coast, the architectural marvels of Florence to the gastronomic delights of Bologna, we've attempted to capture the essence of the Italian experience.

We explored Italy's artistic and architectural treasures that span millennia, shaping our collective history and influencing cultures around the globe. We reveled in the delightful complexity of Italian cuisine, where food is synonymous with celebration, an expression of regional identity, and a testament to the country's bountiful land and seas.

Italy's transportation network, despite occasional unpredictability, has hopefully been demystified, allowing you to navigate the country's roads, rails, and waterways with confidence. We delved into Italy's rich viticulture, tasting our way through the varied wine regions, each with their unique grapes and wine-making traditions.

Through building your itinerary, we trust you now understand how to balance your time, combining iconic sights with local experiences, while leaving room for Italy's famous 'dolce far niente' – the sweetness of doing nothing. We've shared tips on Italian etiquette, helping you blend in with locals and respect the traditions and customs of the land.

Yet, despite the wealth of information, tips, and insights shared, there's still much more to discover about Italy. The real magic often lies in the unexpected, in the moments you leave open to chance. It's in the hospitality of the Italian people, the stories shared, the laughter ringing out in a bustling piazza, and the hidden corners waiting to be discovered.

So, as you set out on your journey, embrace the Italian spirit of 'l'arte di arrangiarsi' – the art of making something out of nothing. Be ready for surprises, be open to new experiences, and most importantly, take the time to enjoy every moment.

In Italy, every journey, every meal, every interaction is an opportunity to create a memory. So, go forth, explore, taste, and soak in the beauty of Italy. And when you're back home, flipping through these pages, may the memories flood back, the tastes linger on your palate, and the sounds echo in your ears.

Arrivederci – until we meet again – Italy is always waiting, ready to welcome you back with open arms and an uncorked bottle of Chianti. Let the thought of that next trip keep your wanderlust alive. After all, as the saying goes, 'Tutte le strade portano a Roma' - All roads lead to Rome!

ABOUT THE AUTHOR

Franco Marzella is a second-generation Italian-American, born and raised in California, with a profound love for Italy. As a seasoned pharmacist by profession, Franco is renowned for his meticulous attention to detail and dedication to service. These qualities permeate his work as a travel writer, where he provides insightful, practical guidance informed by his extensive travels to Italy, both for business and pleasure.

With familial roots in Sicily and Rome, Franco's unique perspective breathes depth and authenticity into his writing. His travel guide "Italy: More than Just a Journey" is the first in a series designed to bring readers closer to the very heart and soul of Italy.

Should you have any questions or comments, please don't hesitate to reach out to Franco at contact@morethanitaly.com. To get a glimpse of his travels and culinary adventures, follow him on Instagram at @pastadoctor. Explore more about Franco, his books, and his love for Italy at his website: www.morethanitaly.com.

Made in the USA
Las Vegas, NV
26 October 2023